INTERIM MANAGEMENT FOR BEGINNERS

AF208620

Marcus Karl HAMAN, MSc

It is never easy to start a new profession

The difference between company consultants and Interim Managers is the conversion
and acceptance of responsibility

Marcus Karl Haman

Marcus Karl HAMAN, MSc

INTERIM MANAGEMENT

FOR BEGINNERS

Production management

for managers

Bibliographic Information of the German National Library (Deutsche Nationalbibliothek):

The German National Library lists this publication in the German National Library; The detailed bibliographical data can be recalled in the internet over http://dnb.dnb.de.

Illustration: **Marcus Karl HAMAN, MSc,**

　　　canstockphoto.at

Further participants: **HCA-consulting GmbH**

Translation: Prakash Chitale

Prepared and published by: BoD– Books on Demand, Norderstedt

ISBN: 9783756852109

MIX
Papier aus verantwortungsvollen Quellen
Paper from responsible sources
FSC® C105338
FSC
www.fsc.org

Contents

INTRODUCTION

Interim Management has grown in several developed countries to an established and acknowledged tool to cover different topics in an organization. The applicability of an Interim Manager is multifold and in tricky as well as in everyday situations it can represent an excellent alternative to own internal resources. Especially when topics, which cannot be found in the portfolio of the core competences of the undertaking have to be dealt with.

Especially in times of crisis, when jobs are being cut and interim managers are in demand, many employees who are looking for a new, professional challenge try to "save themselves" in an interim mandate. However, this is the wrong approach. Interim management is not a "life raft" on which to seek refuge from unemployment, because the challenges of a mandate demand a lot from a manager. Interim manager is a profession like any other, which should be seen as a vocation and should be exercised just as respectfully. The prerequisites are to be seen like a recipe. A lot of experience, extensive skills in different areas, disciplines, and the knowledge of what you can and cannot do.

The reason is that the interim world is very small, and every error is immediately detected and registered.

A distinction must also be made between the types of interim management that individual aspires to or would like to exercise. Simple holiday replacements at clerk level, the supreme discipline at C-level, or anything in between. Every beginning is difficult, even in this profession, but perseverance and determination are also very much in demand here and demand a lot from the candidate.

A certain amount of courage for change is already necessary to include an external manager for the first time in your own organization, however, in most of the cases a clear additional value adjusts itself within the organization through the awarded mandate. In case of a consultation by a management consultant, the concerns are somewhat less, since he need not be included in the organization. In many instances the management consultant has connection only with the Top Management   and he is available to the team only in the training area. Thus, the inhibition threshold is lower, since, as a rule, the management consultant has no access to the company internal data. As against this, the Interim Manager, in order to be able to do justice to his profession and to achieve success, has access to a number of informations and to the employees. However, the Interim Manager also implements steps and thus lines up the proof of his solutions, or he is evaluated by the success or failure of his implementation. Obviously, the Interim Manager is contractually bound to confidentiality and to prohibition against passing on the information by signing a confidentiality agreement.

An Interim Manager brings some advantages with him and depending upon the task given and its area, in a number of instances he saves his costs caused by the mandate. In many instances in a multiple fashion, since with his overall view and his experience, Interim Manager recognizes the unused potentials in an undertaking. Similarly, the Interim Manager develops solutions in order to implement reasonable savings. As many-sided the area of application is, as versatile are the Interim Managers. As example, in Germany everyone who feels called upon for this, can bargain his labor as Interim Manager in the controversial market. In contrast to this, in

Austria, the Interim Manager, who comes under the column management consultant must register his profession and must be allowed by the authorities. In this case it is a regulated profession, which is very strictly controlled by the authorities. Alone the wish to practice the profession does not suffice here. It requires a comprehensive training and a minimum number of years in practice with relevant orientation or reference letters of large undertakings with the job description in order to pass positively the validity check by the authorities. And as in every profession, there is a great amount of variation with respect to capability and competence. Many of them want to practice the profession, however, the competence is absent to carry this out. Here the customer must maintain his standards and keep his eyes open for the search of a suitable Interim Manager in order to separate chaff from wheat. However, in the free job market there are the so-called providers, who happily take over the pre-selection of the suitable candidates. However, there are differences here as well. As a rule, every provider maintains an Interim Manager Pool, which contains a certain number of candidates. Each Interim Manager can register himself with an Interim

Provider and try for inclusion in the Pool. Less good Providers take up every manager for a short period and know their managers only via a CV sent through an E-Mail. Thus, they pass on a relatively unknown person to a customer. As against this the Good Providers know their managers personally over a period and know which candidate fits in to which organization, or the capabilities and competences of the individual managers.

Because one thing must be said: Not every Interim Manager fits in to every undertaking or for every mandate.

So, what really makes a good Interim Manager? Which competences does an Interim Manager need in order to be able to convert a mandate successfully and thus to generate a profit or value for the respective customer? This is a question, which cannot be answered with one sentence. The more individual as the mandate inquiries are, the more complicated it shall be to find the right manager. Therefore, it is important to know the Interim Manager and his capabilities and to deploy these in a proper manner.

With 5 special questions to the Interim Manager the decision-making of the customer can perhaps be made somewhat easier.

THE 5 QUESTIONS ABOUT INTERIM MA-NAGEMENT

Apart from the question regarding experience and as to how many mandates the manager has successfully completed, there are essentially 5 questions, which a good Interim Manager does not fail in and offers to the customer the opportunity to get to know the manager somewhat better in course of time. Although nothing is more important than experience, the competence and the culture of the manager are also important factors on the way to success.

The importance of the questions also consists in representing the deployment ability and the improvement of the organization through an Interim Manager.

Because one thing is certain: the right Interim Manager can bring a considerable value to an organization.

THE 5 QUESTIONS ARE:

What does an interim
manager stand for?

Which work topics
are covered by the
Interim manager?

How does an
interim manager
work?

Which competences
does an interim
manager need?

How does an
interim manager
proceed?

QUESTION 1: WHAT DOES THE INTERIM MANAGER STAND FOR?

For a customer, an Interim Manager at the first step causes costs. The requirement of the customer consists in the fact that required topics are successfully carried out or realized without causing irritation or discomfort within the team of the undertaking. Therefore, it is important on the one hand to increase the confidence level in the undertaking and on the other hand to support this confidence with activities and competence.

The „foreign body "called Interim Manager is taken notice of within the entire organization and everything that the Interim Manager undertakes is evaluated and discussed by the team. Therefore, especially at the beginning of each mandate the mode of operation is so to be adjusted that it does not come to an irritation and to a consequent standstill in the organization.

THE INTERIM MANAGER SHOULD OB-SERVE 5 POINTS:

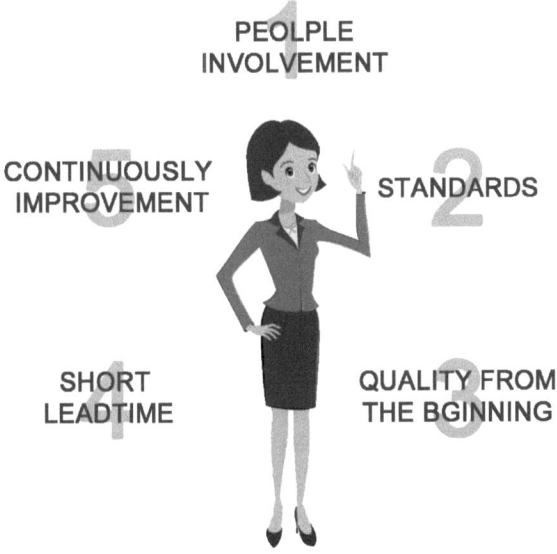

PEOLPLE INVOLVEMENT

CONTINUOUSLY IMPROVEMENT

STANDARDS

SHORT LEADTIME

QUALITY FROM THE BGINNING

1. Inclusion of all the colleagues

As a rule, the inclusion of all the colleagues prevents uncertainties and acts against the fears within the team. If the colleagues are not regularly and pro-actively informed about the objective, on the one hand an envy group is formed, since only privileged employees are allowed to participate in the ‚secrets' and the ‚rest' can be left dumb. On the other hand, there are fears about the working place and about the connected social security. Thus, unconsciously the security thinking, which every employee carries within himself, is strengthened and other capacities and priorities are classified as not so important anymore, or they are pushed back. The thinking of safety takes over the command, the employees modify their behavior and as a rule they bring lower performance and unconsciously more mistakes. Thus, a negatively aligned spiral gets going, which can be stopped only with a lot of expense and effort. The countermeasure to this is to involve all the employees proactively.

Many a projects and changes fail due to (lack of) communication and not due to the competence of the employees.

However, how does the Interim Manager ensure the inclusion of all the employees?
With his capability of adaptation, the Interim Manager should be able to follow the guiding principle of the undertaking and in order that his measures do justice to the vision and the values of the customer organization, in so far as this is still possible. Thus, employees are not irritated still more, and they find themselves in the familiar topics.
Similarly, it is important, even the first priority, to place the employees in the foreground, in that the Interim Manager places great value on work safety and environment. A safe place of work and the assurance is necessary that all the employees leave the company at least as healthy as they have entered it, and this is achieved in the organization.
Besides the open communication and the demonstration of the team concept, with corresponding performance and results, the recognition of these has high importance for the employee. Who would not like to be praised and held in high esteem for his

performance? The last point is very important not only for the employee on the shop floor but also in other areas of the undertaking – the presence „at site ". The Interim Manager must show presence and support at site. He must be seen to actively perceive the „pains" and requirements of the organization in the core business.

2. Standards

Standards are the essential parts in the exercise of a mandate. However, this does not mean that the Interim Manager takes over a new mandate and uses his rigid methods and systems, since these led to success in a different project. The Interim Manager takes during his journey into a mandate a toolbox filled with methods and systems, which with his experience he adapts to the undertaking and individually customizes to the requirements of the mandate. Also, not all the methods, systems and standards fit in to every organization. The Interim Manager with his experience and competence must sensibly consider, as to which tools and standards he can deploy. Similarly, the Interim Manager should not chase after the symptoms. The Interim Manager must rather concentrate on the real causes and fighting them. The Interim Manager analyses and employs standards, which bring forward the undertaking and experience a higher value through this. The advantages are obvious here. Through the standards the training phases at the place of work are enormously reduced or the error costs are considerably cut down.

By means of standardization, as for instance error lists to the Team Info Tables on shopfloor, the potentials in the area of processes and savings become clearly visible.

Standards as for example SABs (Standardized Work Sheet), standardized workplace descriptions, forms, key figures, plans of measures, and many other things, help the organization to become more transparent and to make errors more visible, which in turn with full support of all participants can be efficiently and effectively minimized.

Essentially a number of instruments and topics for the improvement of the organization are available in a mandate in the theme heading. Topics like the workplace organization, the time management, the standardized working and the visual management.

interim management for beginners

3. Quality from the beginning

Quality is not only with reference to and applicable to products. Moreover, and especially in case of interim mandates, the quality of action and of implementation, or of the procedure and of the action in the mandate within the customer organization is important. Earlier it was called the „Handshake Quality "in order to comply with oral agreements and understandings. Today contracts are made and signed for sealing. In a number of cases the trigger in a mandate is a tricky situation. The more clear is the claim to influence „qualitatively" in the organization, to adhere to the agreements, to practice exemplary procedures and to match the mode of work to the undertaking. The capability of integration is similarly decisive for the success and should not be confused with "a cuddling course". In many instances the Interim Mandates have the wishes for modification of the Top Management as their objective. Unpleasant situations and decisions must be executed or converted in a mandate. The Interim Manager is, especially at the beginning, a disturbance factor for the team and in the eyes of the colleagues, he represents a risk. Thus, the team members perhaps do not behave very openly, and they behave rather reservedly with respect to passing on of information. Here it is important to prove both the fine touch as also the assertiveness and to get the team on ‚board‘. Here the quality of action is a significant factor. In most of the cases the straight-line behavior and exemplary effect do help to make the soil good on the stony path to receive respect within the organization.

The art to convince through actions and not only through words without the team breaking away and chaos being created is the demand from an Interim Manager.

Theme areas, which the Interim Manager can use for improvements and for achieving the objective, are for instance:

- Quality standards for products
- Validation of the manufacturing processes
- Process monitoring and control
- Quality reporting system along the entire delivery chain and
- The Quality management system

4. Short lead time

In case of short run periods the production man immediately thinks about the manufacture of components, however, even in case of Interim Mandates, there is the claim of a short run period. It is on the one hand with respect to the run period of the mandate and on the other hand in the processing of the tasks and the promised obligations of the Interim Manager. Each mandate causes costs and at first view it presents a stress on the budget. Therefore, the organization of the customer is trying to fix the mandate as short as possible. This view changes itself with the number of observed and analyzed saving potentials by the Interim Manager, in so far as the Top Management decides also to perceive these potentials.

In many cases, when the Interim Manager carries out his tasks, works out savings and implements these successfully, the customer recognizes the value of the contribution by the Interim Manager and extends the mandate on his own, since the customer recognizes that the step works out.

The possibilities of the Interim Manager to generate savings in the field of short run periods for the customer are manifold. These are topics like the following, which the Interim Manager can take "under the magnifying glass" in a mandate.

- Simple material flow
- Small packing sizes
- Fixed order cycles
- Controlled external transport
- Planned material dispatch and receipt
- Temporary material stores
- Need oriented material delivery (Pull System)
- Uniform programme
- Logistc management system

However, it should be remembered that multi-front wars are not sensible for fighting waste and that the organization can break or that the team cannot follow any more. To take up one topic after the other is more effective.

5. Continuous improvement

The continuous improvement process is not a new thought; however, this should also be considered in case of every mandate. This involves the sustainability of the introduced or implemented measures by the Interim Manager. Especially when he leaves the mandate, there should be no vacuum, nor a gap should be left behind. Continuous improvement and further development of the undertaking in holistic view is essential and must be correspondingly treated or attempted. Under this also comes the knowledge transfer and a basic training for the topic CIP (continuous improvement process) to the employees, should the organization not have implemented any CIP strategy as yet. The Interim Manager has thus the task to align the undertaking with full assistance of the Top Management (Customer), in the direction of continuous further development and improvement in all disciplines.

However, which topics can the Interim Manager tackle with the organization in the field of CIP (continuous improvement process)?

Topics like structured problem solution, Business Plan Deployment (Key figure system and travel plans of the Organization), slim design for equipment, facilities, tools and layout, as well as a preventive maintenance (TPM) and the CIP as process and project development are mighty tasks which can be taken up by the Interim Manager.

QUESTION 2: HOW DOES AN INTERIM MANAGER WORK?

Due to the time pressure prevailing in many mandates to achieve the agreed upon objectives, the experienced Interim Manager should use the following 5 functioning methods:

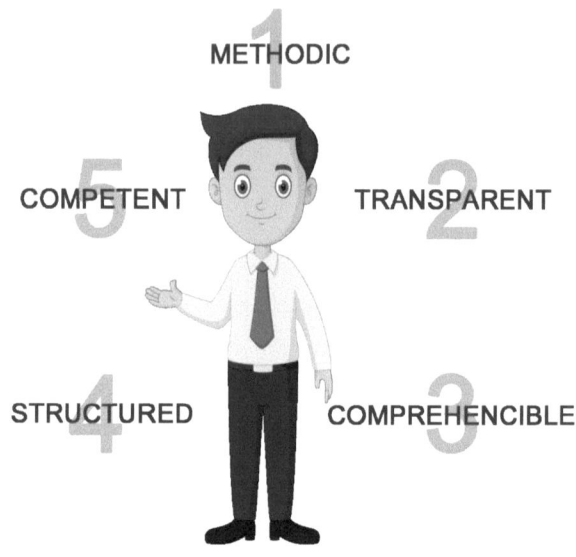

1. Methodical

The advantage of an Interim Manager is that he brings along a lot of experience with methods and systems, however, he also is capable of knowledge transfer and of efficient implementation. Methodical approach is indispensable for efficient implementation of the measures and for steps of change in order to be able to ensure the success for the client.

These are not newly invented, but rather long tested methods, which in part must be matched to the respective situation and organization.

Methods like for instance:

- 6S
- 7 Types of waste
- Containment
- VSM – value stream analysis
- TOC – theory of constraints
- And many others

2. Transparent

Transparent working hides two types of aspects in itself. On the one hand the functioning is visible for all, and problems or errors are immediately recognized and perceived by all participants. Thus, at the beginning the Interim Manager as well as the relevant department are under pressure and must endure certain criticism. Also, within the organization it is perhaps not always desired by all participants or affected employees to represent everything transparently. However, transparent action in the mandate ensures a high speed of implementation. When problems come openly „on the table", nobody can discuss them away and corresponding measures are implemented, visible to all. Responsibilities are clearly defined, and deadlines given. Thus, everyone is asked to carry out his assigned and agreed upon part of the work in time and in totality. Also, the support from Top Management, if required, is thus claimed and decisions must be made. Since these agreements are also accessible for everyone in the undertaking in the form of measures / countermeasures, these are as a rule hung on a Teamboard on the Shopfloor.

Therefore, there are no reasons not to work these out or to forget them unintentionally. Should however there are reasons which speak against a timely implementation then these are transparently communicated and countermeasures against these are introduced.

3. Comprehensible

Measures, which were not implemented in a comprehensible manner, are not existent.

A problem is only then solved, and the cause found, when the problem can be switched on and off in a targeted manner, whenever and as often as required.

The pre-requisite for this is however the traceability of the solution.

Situations, wherein something was implemented, however no one knows why and how, are dangerous, since the situations can escalate once again and nobody has the knowledge, how to get rid of the cause efficiently and immediately in a durable manner.

interim management for beginners

4. Structured

The Interim Manager knows his approach and could immediately implement many measures, however, not successfully, since the sustainability would be available in the least number of cases. It is therefore important to „fetch" the team and to accompany it on the way to implementation. The Interim Manager should not proceed from his knowledge. He must find a basis, from which the team can follow the Interim Manager. Structured approach is here decisive for the success. The more structured and the more accomplishable the individual steps of the Interim Manager are, the earlier shall be the understanding and support from the team of the undertaking.

Structures simplify complex measures and processes and can thus be conveyed quicker and more effectively on a broad basis.

5. Competent

Without expertise an implementation of the agreed upon customer objectives shall be difficult, however, expertise is not the only competence that the Interim Manager has to bring into the respective mandate. The Interim Manager must be able in the shortest possible period. to win the respect and confidence of the team, since otherwise the Interim Manager shall have difficulties to execute his mandate successfully. Respect and confidence cannot be purchased in the supermarket of the Interim Managers, much rather these must be hard earned. To convince through competence, however not with arrogance and overbearing is a very effective way. Paired with social competence and directness a team can be convinced to pull on together and to approach proactively or openly the steps of modification and to support these.

QUESTION 3: HOW DOES AN INTERIM MANAGER PROCEED?

Every mandate requires a set of rules in order to define clearly the requirements of the customer and agreed upon tasks of the Interim Manager. Similarly, it is necessary to implement a comprehensible and transparent procedure, to which both the customer as also all the participants and especially the affected employees of respective organization can orient themselves.

The 5-step method offers such a possibility, and it is successfully implemented in several cases.

THE 5 STEPS ARE:

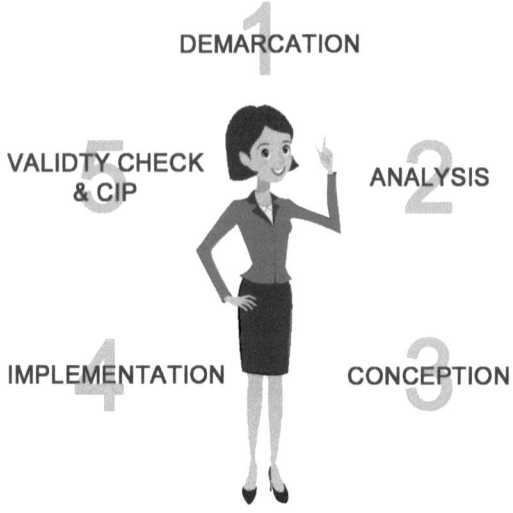

DEMARCATION

ANALYSIS

CONCEPTION

IMPLEMENTATION

VALIDTY CHECK & CIP

Step 1: DEMARCATION

The delimitation in a mandate is essential for the customer as also for the Interim Manager, since in a delimitation the following points can be clearly defined:

- Roles & responsibillities (RASI Chart)
- In scope / out of scope
- Budget (in case of investments)
- Contributors
- Objective / intermediate objectives
- Schedule
- Resources plan
- etc.

1. DEMARCATION

Contracts and delimitations/agreements are concluded in order to prevent misunderstandings in the communication and to express clearly the expectations of the customer on the one hand and the powers and rules of the Interim Manager on the other hand.

The delimitation also serves as checklist in a mandate around the path to success or in order not to lose sight of the objective.

Success is said to have come, when the customer is at least satisfied, however, enthusiasm on part of the party taking the mandate should be striven for.

Step 2: ANALYSIS

In the analysis the findings of the Interim Manager are placed transparently on the „table". Through the transparent mode of working the mandate becomes transparent and can be criticized however, on the other side it opens up the possibility of full support of the entire team, inclusive of the Top Management, to use the potentials within the organization and also to use the potentials in order to strengthen the market position. Many decision makers or top managers are perhaps not so enthusiastic to make everything so transparent, because it involves their area of responsibility. Good top managers use this possibility to perceive the unused potentials for the further development. The success remains with the top manager, because the Interim Manager leaves, as the name already says, the undertaking after a specific period and the top manager can then pursue further the path of success.

Top Managers, who permit transparent work-ing, are performance oriented and should be fully supported and strengthened to take this path further, even if actions follow the imple-mentation.

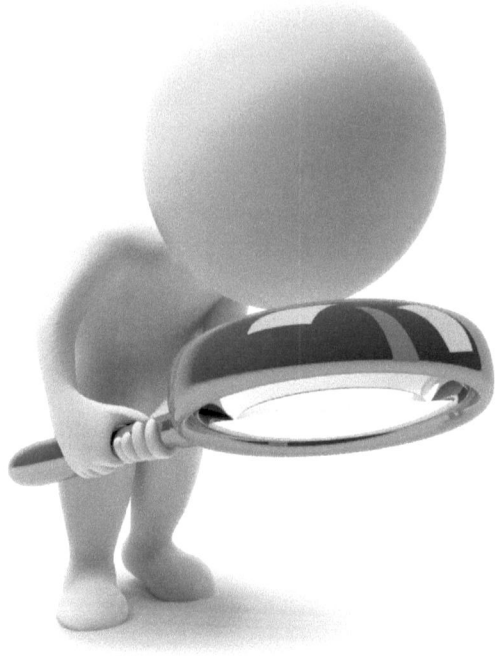

Step 3: CONCEPTION

In the concept the analyzed figures, data and facts, which are provided with measures and detailed agreements of objectives, which in turn are supplemented with clear responsibility and a timeline, are put in writing. Preferably the measure charts, which are hung in the organization, should contain these not very confidential data and measures. This step requires a lot of time and effort, however, the more exact and the more defined or considered and detailed the measures packages are, the lesser are the discussions, delays and surprises in the implementation phase.

Also the so-called „Contingency Plans" to the concept phase, which only show an objective – to clarify the following question „What do we do. When this or that does not take place or fails? ". These continuation plans are a part of a risk evaluation, which should not be missing in any mandate. It should be decided case by case, whether a Basic Risk Assessment (BRA) or a Full Risk Assessment (FRA) is to be used.

Step 4: IMPLEMENTATION

In the implementation phase for the Interim Manager, rather an advisory and controlling function is attributed. The implementation itself should be carried out in the team. The reason for this lies in the fact that the colleagues, who are involved or affected in the modification process, criticize their implementation the least; they shall much rather support these modifications through their joint decision-making and involvement/participation in the concept phase and defend them against the skeptics. Therefore, the involvement of all colleagues in the organization is an important constituent on the way to success.

The role and responsibility in this step-in case of Interim Manager lies in the fact that as already mentioned above he is available as advisor and for control, however, the Interim Manager takes over the leadership, when negative deviations to the should-target become visible or to claim the processing. He remains a „care-taker" of the decided measures and of their timely processing.

Step 5: VALIDITY CHECK & CIP (Continuous improvement process)

Even when the Top Management or the leadership has faith in the employees, control mechanisms are important, in order not to lose sight of the agreed upon targets. A scrutiny as to where the implementation of agreed upon measures stands at certain points of time prevents in many instances the failure of the modification. The main task of the validity check lies in counteracting against countermeasures in case of undesired changes. The longer is the time interval of the status scrutiny of the measures, the longer it lasts to implement the corrective measures in case of negative modification and to take up the desired course once again.

As a rule, new potentials become visible during the implementation, which should be similarly taken up in the list of measures, in order to ensure a continuous further development. The improvement process never ends, especially for the Interim Manager, and it must be continuously and sustainably driven forward or promoted.

The basis of the procedure forms the base of the PDCA circle method, which is very well-known especially in the automotive industry or is practiced there.

QUESTION 4: WHICH COPETENCES / CAPABILITIES ARE REQUIRED BY AN INTERIM MANAGER?

The Interim Manager requires more than only one competence in order to successfully implement the mostly demanding demands of the customer.

PROFESSIONAL COMPETENCE & EXPERIENCE

SOCIAL COMPETENCE

ANALYTICAL THINKING

STRATEGY & VISIONARY THINKING

IMPLEMENTATION POWER

1. Professional competence & experience

The basic requirements for exercising the profession of Interim Manager certainly are competence and experience. The reason lies in the necessary speed to implement professionally the measures for achieving the objective and to settle down in the respectively prevailing situation. Through the several years of experience in different fields and organizations, the Interim Manager has been able to collect experience and if possible, implement a number of times for the respective undertaking, profitably whenever possible. The competences of an Interim Manager are certainly not only of professional nature. Rather factors like personality, strength of implementation and social competence are necessary, when there are tricky problems, which need to be solved speedily. Seen from the training angle, the Interim Manager trains himself further continuously and steadily after his studies. It may be through courses, events or with every new mandate. Should the situation require it, the Interim Manager can recall this diversity of knowledge in every mandate at any given time. The situation has to require it. The Interim Manager has a large box, full of methods, systems and standards during every mandate and depending upon the mandate and situation, he can use the right tools in order to deal with the mandate.

2. Analytical thinking capacity

An important strength to accompany the respective mandate effectively and efficiently is certainly the analytical thinking capacity of the Interim Manager. The Manager does not know the organization, in which the changes are desired. However, he must analyze the situations and possibilities and work out measures in the shortest possible period or implement them. This cannot be achieved without the competence of the analytical thinking capacity.

Analytical thinking capacity describes the capability to recognize and to solve problems.

Essentially the analytical thinking capacity can be subdivided into the following points:

- Problem detection / comprehension
- Breakdown in to part aspects
- Strategies for problem solution

3. Implementing power

In order to act successfully in a mandate and to generate the results agreed upon with the customer, the implementing power of the respective Interim Manager is the pre-requisite.

Implementing power also includes enforcing capacity, however, not only provided hierarchically, but rather interdisciplinary and with social competence. The Interim Manager must be able to „pick up" the team and to accompany it or to guide it to the result. Implementing power has nothing to do with short term „whipping" and execution of measures with pressure. The implementing power can be much rather understood as implementation of measures without social loss and friction on material base with clear focus on the essentials – the achieving of agreed upon objectives.

4. Strategy & Vision capability

Interim Managers know after a short period as to where the organization in mandate is located. Thus, in agreement with the customer target agreements can be agreed upon. Through the vast experience of the Interim Manager, he is in a position to see a „target image" where the mandate should or/and must lead. This picture is missing in most of the organizations, since the employees display long period relationships and due to that do not know anything else than their own work environment.

How should someone draw a sketch of the Eifel Tower, when he has never seen it as yet.

The Interim Manager requires a picture or the imagination, as to where the respective mandate can be led or should be led. He must then be able to convey this picture as achievable vision/target to the Top Management and the employees. A strategy shows the path to reaching the target or fulfillment of the vision. As against this a vision shows an ideal picture of the achievable. Whether this is called target or project vision has little relevance. However, the language of communication should be matched to the respective organization.

5. Social competence

In many projects the social competence remains as a withered corpse with low significance in a dark cell, An Interim Manager cannot make a mistake bigger than this. The social competence is essential in achieving the target, because one thing is certain from the beginning:

Without the team, namely the team of the respective organization, the Interim Manager cannot implement sustainably anything, except the closure of a location.

Therefore, it is essential to find this capability in an Interim Manager or to scrutinize it. Without „taking along" and „inclusion" of the employees, most of the mandates are destined to fail. As an example, the following case may be described:

An Interim Manager is used in a tricky situation and has the task as works manager to increase the throughput. In other words, to increase the productivity with the same number of employees. The Interim Manager divides the target with the directly reporting lead personnel and demands their implementation. So far, so good. What he had however forgotten was to inform the managers, how to do this. In addition to this the Interim Manager went to a nearby parking lot and photographed the workers standing around and noted down the break timings, in order to discuss these loudly with the managers. The communication on the shopfloor was not an option, because the Interim Manager had never found the way to the production department, namely to the core process.

This is certainly an absolute horror example of the execution of an Interim Mandate. However, there are unfortunately such Interim Managers as well. The result was that the productivity went down, since the employees had no motivation, they were not involved and not evaluated. The Interim Manager was changed at short notice and substituted by another Interim Manager, who did not have it exactly easy to transform the scorched earth once again into a green meadow.

How would be the solution with social competence? The approach of the second Interim Manager was the following:

- Introduction to the whole team
- Presence on the shopfloor
- Support of the team
- Promoting of and demanding from the team
- Inclusion of all the employees
- Target agreements and reviews worked out with the team
- Employee discussions with the directly reporting management personnel
- Regular discussions on the shopfloor for achieving the target
- Appreciation of the employees through support and help or requests and pro-active communication
- Transparent action
- Consistent implementation
- etc.

Certainly, it is not simply these points that are to be implemented or deployed, however, the effort is worth it, and the success makes the above-mentioned points right. Social competence should never be underestimated and certainly not be neglected, if the organization is aspiring a successful implementation.

QUESTION 5: WHICH WORK TOPICS ARE COVERED BY THE INTERIM MANAGER IN A MANDATE?

An Interim Manager is often deployed very selectively in an organization. However, the Interim Manager may attend more than only one topic. It makes sense for the customer to deploy the Interim Manager in totality and to consider his work area with his experience and expertise. Depending upon the mandate assignment and level, in which the Interim Manager is deployed, the Interim Manager can generate value for the customer and stumble upon saving potentials and process modifications or also implement them.

The following topics refer not only to manufacturing undertakings or reflect on the department for production. Also, a marketing department or other departments of the undertaking can be considered with the 5 topics.

DIE 5 THE AREAS ARE:

HEALTH & SAFETY ENVIRONMENT

PEOPLE

QUALITY

COST

PRODUCTIVITY

1. Health & safety and environment

Work safety and environment refer to the highest possession in the undertaking, namely the employee, in the most direct manner and should thus assume the highest priority and value in the organization. Many improvement projects can be encountered here, not only in the production department. Just as in all other topics, here also cost savings, like the reduction of absentee days, stand in the focus, only to mention one topic.

With method and structure, also in the area of work safety and environment sensible savings can be made. As example, here not only the reduction of the work accidents and the related absentees of the individual employees are mentioned as saving potential. Also mentioned are costs for garbage separation and the corresponding disposal costs.

2. Quality

Quality is always seen as product quality; however, it is much more. Quality of the work, of the action and the dealing with the customer also stand here in center.

A sales example for cost saving under the topic quality:

A customer orders a product from the sales department. The Sales Department gives this information erroneously in to an internal ordering system and the production department manufactures the product according to the details given by the internal sales department, however, not as desired by the customer. For this example, there are a few improvement approaches, however, the trigger is an activity of the internal sales department which was not correctly executed with respect to quality. Through this in turn costs are incurred and they endanger the profits and the market position. The Interim Manager recognizes and analyses these processes and possibilities of causing error, and if desired by the customer these can be changed by the Interim Manager. Here the outside view and the experience of the manager do help.

3. Productivity

In the core business of production an outside view and a profound level of experience and knowledge of implementation of an Interim Manager is very profitable. Because, from the several successfully implemented mandates, he indeed knows sufficient possibilities to bring about an improvement. However, it is true here as well: depending upon the area of application and level of the Interim Manager, even other areas of the topic of production can be analyzed with respect to saving potentials and improvements. It is not only the Production Department that produces. A sales department generates assignments. Exactly considered, in case of process there are scarcely any differences between a production department and a sales department. Both the departments produce and can be represented in a process chain. In the sales department an order is accepted and processed further. Then it is maintained in a system and calculated, taxed and after delivery it is accounted. Many process steps, which the order runs through, till it becomes a „Product", which is called Order.

4. Costs

The topic costs are referred to in every topic and it is found in every field. Every act and action can be represented in terms of costs. Thus, these topics can be subjected also to a savings analysis by the Interim Manager with external view, who, with his experience knows or could know a lot of organizations. In particular the Interim Manager can show and reduce product costs, error costs, headcount costs and every type of wastage. Seen figuratively, the Interim Manager can be seen as hunter on wastage hunt in the process jungle.

5. Organization development

A sensitive topic in an organization is certainly the development of organization. It is not only a personnel topic which causes efforts to the personnel department. Much rather it is an operative topic, which can lead to the motivation or frustration of the employees. The employees often feel to have been treated unfairly. May it be through the pay reduction of the position of the task area and of the further development of the respective worker. Here a number of personal aspects and sensitivities play a role.

The Interim Manager knows and master's methods and systems in order to tackle these topics professionally and to work out solutions. The implementation then takes place together with the responsible party within the organization, as for instance within the personnel department.

The Interim Manager should never be perceived as risk in the organization. An Interim Manager is a part of the organization only for a specific period and can generate a value in the undertaking in many areas. It is important that there is a clear communication and that the full support of the Top management is available.

WHICH APPLICATION AREAS ARE THERE FOR AN INTERIM MANAGER?

For which topics interim mandates are given, which topics and areas can an external manager take over and which can be profitably introduced for the undertaking of the customer? There are many possibilities of use for an Interim Manager. In a number of cases the lead positions are occupied by an Interim Manager. In order to be able to work successfully, the Interim Manager requires „free Hand", that is flexibility of action, which was clearly agreed upon in advance with the client. Without having the reins in hand, the Interim Manager can take up only a secondary role or be active as advisor.

The 5 Application Areas of an Interim Manager are:

1. Absence of a key person

He decides every day anew for or with whom and what he would like to work.

Thus, with the exit of a manager, undertakings are required to keep the negative effect as low as possible. On the one hand, so that the daily business is not affected, and on the other hand, in order not to allow any unrest to prevail within the team. When the manager himself decides to leave the undertaking, there is always the question, whether the adherence to the termination period is sensible, or whether it is better to make free the manager immediately or within a short period. In case of misconduct of the manager, the question does not arise, and an immediate termination is essential. In this case, the deployment of an immediately available Interim Manager is very much required, indeed because he can indeed contain the arising unrest and can close the gap formed to the greatest possible extent. In most of the cases, he is not the product specialist in the undertaking, however, there is the question, whether he must be this as well, in order to conduct further the daily business as the leader.

2. Change-management

Organizations, which subject themselves to a modification process or plan the same, are well advised to subject themselves to an external inspection. In one's own „soup" not all potentials are recognized and thus the possibilities to develop the organization further are not perceived. Here an Interim Manager helps, who can bring in his knowledge not only through his multi-year and international experience. Thus, he can convey a picture, as to how it could look in the future. He also efficiently implements the desired modification with the team. In a number of cases, it is good to consult an external manager, since he can approach the change factually and unbiased and without historical prejudice.

3. Vacancy bridgeover

The search for a suitable candidate in a succession scheme is difficult and tedious in a number of cases. Since the claim of the undertaking is high and the desired image of the new manager in the undertaking is clear for the organization, it can sometimes take longer to find the suitable candidate in the empty job market. In order not to have to spend this period without a guiding person, an Interim Manager can help. He immediately takes over the position or accompanies the employee going away in order to take over his functions and knowledge and remains so long in the undertaking, till a new candidate is found. The Interim Manager through his experience can also support in the selection of the new candidate through his independent outside view. A vacancy support role with an Interim Manager is also sensible due to the possible daily termination, since he can be flexibly employed without risk.

4. Restructuring & rehabilitation

When companies have come into a difficult situation, then good advice is difficult to come by. The Management is perhaps partly changed by the owners and the pressure by banks and creditors shall become higher day by day. In such situations an Interim Manager can help actively with his long years of experience and especially operatively to either renovate the undertaking or to lead it to a restructuring. Tricky situations require sensible decisions, so that the undertaking handles and survives also the severe measures without great losses. Experience with capability for strategy and vision are two of several capabilities, which the Interim Manager has in his portfolio. It is indeed important to hold the affected customers, suppliers and employees and to bring the undertaking once again on „track". Whether negotiations with the banks or creditors, the use of an external expert in the form of an interim mandate, is seen positively by most of the creditors and as a rule the negotiations are carried out more factually as a rule.

5. Takeover & sale

During a takeover or sale it is essential „to do the right things and to do the things rightly". What sounds so simple can lead to massive impacts after signing the contract. To mention only one topic from several, which is often underestimated.

Due Diligence

Due Diligence denotes a careful examination, which is carried out as a rule, initiated by the buyer, during the purchase of company shareholdings or real estate, as also during an initial public offer or IPO.

This also includes official orders and regulations, ownership rights, contract-relevant agreements and many more.

In most of the cases, this type of experience and competence is absent in undertakings. The experienced Interim Manager with his competence especially in operative area can support to prevent financial damages to the customer.

Similarly, takeover and sale, even though they are kept quite secret, through rumors and speculations, cause irritations and unrest within the organization. Here one must act against this proactively with social competence or in advance a clear strategy of communication must be worked out. It is important here to act against the fears of the employees, to act against exits of key employees and experts/knowledge specialists. The Interim Manager, through his experience from various mandates, has the possibility to bring himself in to this topic competently.

HOW AN INTERIM MANAGER CALCULATES HIS COST?

The question, whether an Interim Manager calculates his cost, engages the decision makers intensively, especially since they are responsible for adherence to the budget of their area of responsibility. In many instances the situations in the organization come to bear effect, which would explain an Interim Mandate to be sensible, however, does not reflect or plan these costs in the budget. Thus, the question poses itself, whether this budget risk can be carried and be answered. During the sale or new purchase of an under-taking, these costs can be planned. During the exit of an employee in management this situation comes rather unplanned on the ta-ble of the daily challenges. Thus, the question is posed, how an Interim Manager could cal-culate his cost.

There are essentially 5 points, which speak in favor of use of an Interim Manager,

The 5 points are:

SAVING POTENTIALS
THROUGH OUTER VIEW

SHORT TERM
CHEAPER THAN
PERMANENT
EMPLOYMENT

IMPROVES
PROCESSES

IMMEDIATELY
AVAILABLE & CAN
BE TERMINATED

COSTS WHICH
CAN BE PLANED

1. Finds Saving potentials through external view

Through the external view and the experience, the Interim Manager has the possibility to consider the undertaking with other „eyes". He is unbiased and displays no blindness for specialization or undertaking. Thus, he is in a position to recognize and perceive saving potentials, which cannot be recognized any more internally. Similarly, he is not in any dependency network within the system. He has no pre-history and can thus on the material level show without bias unused potentials and possibilities as well as organizational errors and improve them or disconnect them.

2. Improves processes through lean methods

In his mandate the Interim Manager also questions the process map and shows mal-administration's and improvement potentials. Especially as regards the topic Lean Management, the Interim Manager can bring in his whole experience from other mandates and profitably implement it for the customer. Many undertakings have long-time employees in their organization, who have grown up in the undertaking. This has certainly advantages, since they know the products and processes very well. However, this is also the main reason of a standstill in the organization with reference to further development and about viewing „over the edge of the box"

How should someone describe the Eiffel Tower, if he has never seen it?

The employee knows his work surroundings like no other, however, perhaps the long-term employee misses the picture, as it would look with improvements. Here the Interim Manager can actively support and can let his entire experience flow along. In contrast to the company advisor, the Interim Manager shows not only the possibilities but also implements these with the team and thus lines up the proof of his solution proposals. Even though the concept Lean in some undertakings is called a curse, the lean methods have their quite clear justification, and they should be intensively used to improve oneself continuously and sustainably.

3. Predictable costs / no failure costs

Since the Interim Manager is only paid, when he works for the customer, these costs can be planned. There are neither failure costs due to sickness or other planned and un-planned absence costs, like vacation, official trips, doctor visits etc. Also, no tax aspects must be considered. Thus, at the end of the month there are no surprises, and the perfor-mance of the Interim Manager is in fore-ground.

4. Immediately available / services can be terminated any day

If it comes to the absence of a Manager or of another employee, then there is a gap. This should be closed as quickly as possible. Search of personnel, depending on the level, can already cost a couple of month's time (as a rule 3-6 months). Here the Manager Pools of the Interim Providers help. These maintain a portfolio of contractual partners, who can be employed within a short period. It is then for the Provider to fish out the right candidate in the „Pool" and present him to the customer. Good providers know their managers personally in course of time and can thus respond specifically to the requirements of the customer with the suitable candidate. It is essential for the mandate as well as for the Interim Provider to select the right manager and to present him, since indeed the name and the reputation of the Provider is on the testing stand for every mandate. Should however there be circumstances, in which the customer conveys his dissatisfaction, then the cooperation with the Interim Manager can be terminated on any day and can be substituted through another candidate. The training time of an Interim Employee cannot be compared with the training time of a new regular employee. Interim Mandates make the claim that the Interim Managers carry out their work at the customer's efficiently, effectively and competently. The proverbial 100 days of incorporation is definitely not there in the Interim Mandate.

5. In the short term more convenient than the fixed employees

In the first step many potential customers are scared by the costs of the Interim Manager. However, if the customer analyses the costs, he shall determine that an Interim Mandate is more cost-saving for short-term appointments than a fixed employment. Neither advertising nor „Headhunter-"costs are incurred. Also, the handling charges are not a topic in case of Interim Mandate. Also, there are no wage costs and labor costs. If these costs are considered, then the decision, whether any or not any mandate is considered, goes clearly in favor of the mandate. As already mentioned, saving potentials and process improvements for implementation come into consideration and change the cost landscape of an Interim Mandate. And each day, on which a manager is missing, is a day, where unused potentials are probably not perceived, and the team is without a leader.

The remuneration of an interim manager is a very important issue when deciding to practice this profession and in many cases the reason and justification to take this career path. Although money plays an essential role, this should not be the only basis for decision-making, because nothing is given to you in this profession.

There are 2 different types of payment. The hourly billing and a daily flat rate. There are many "pros and cons" in the consideration, but from a certain level of responsibility, the question no longer arises because only daily rates are applied.

The question of how high this daily rate, or the hourly rate, may be, is a very delicate one. Asking too much and the customer jumps off. Too little is demanded and the mandate giver says "It's too cheap, it can't do anything".

So it's quite hard to hit the right bandwidth. But as a rule, the amount of the daily or hourly rates depends on what experience the interim manager has and how much responsibility he is given. Equally important is where the mandate will take place. Travel activities and inpatient stays must also be considered here. The amount also depends on which company is in which industry, or how great the need is. So many factors that should be considered.

A project manager mandate in a medium-sized company will be able to charge around 80 euros per hour. A plant manager comes to a daily rate of about 1000 euros per day, whereby it must be considered that working days do not include 8 hours, but rather 10 hours are seen as standard. A mandate position in C-level is valued from 1200 euros.

All the above information is indicative and does not include any claim to the amount. Normally, no travel expenses / expenses, such as flight, km money or accommodation costs are included in the daily rate, or in the hourly rate.

Of course, this sounds very fine, but it must be clearly mentioned that, depending on the country, the tax hits quite heavily.

It should also be mentioned that it is not easy to get the first orders transferred. A great deal of work is required here. Direct mandates are extremely rare and the path via a provider / intermediary will not be missing.

HOW DO I GET MANDATES?

Obtaining mandates is a very competitive area and the interim company is very manageable. There are about 80,000 interim managers in German-speaking countries. That sounds a lot, but many management consultants, who drive the number very upwards, are included here.

And then not all interim managers, for example, work in production or finance. Thus, the number of available for certain topics is getting smaller and smaller. Thus, the individual providers know the candidates and exchange some information. This has advantages and disadvantages, because if the interim manager produces mistakes, or "flies" out of a mandate, not much will happen the first time, but the second or even the third time, it will be rather tight, as the provider endangers his reputation and thus is more likely to mediate another manager and drop the "hot" potato.

Performance is everything!

Which provider the individual manager chooses is up to him if he is also willing to include the new manager in his portfolio.

In most cases, there is an admission process, which is used here. But there is also a wide range of quality among the providers.

Some providers only want to sell the managers and know them only partially, others want to get to know the candidate properly, i.e., personally, and design the multi-stage admission process into the interim pool, complex and like a job interview or an assessment.

The choice is then on both sides, but it is recommended to visit several providers and register / be recorded.

Interim Manager Providers can be found very easily on Google & Co.

NOTES

ABBREVIATIONS / LEGEND:

BPD	Business Plan Deployment
EDMI	Decision, Execution, Participation, Information
FTQ	First Time Quality
OEE	Total Machine Efficiency
HR	Human Resources
IT	Information Technology
KPI	Key Performance Indicator
CIP	Continuous Improvement Process
ME	Manufacturing Engineering
NA	Not Available
PDCA	Plan Do Check Act
PKB	Problem Communication Sheet
QM	Quality Management
RASI	Responsible Action Support Information
TIC	Team Info Center
TPM	Total Productive Maintenance
Shop-floor	Work Area in the Production

Further Publications

5 Regeln der Produktion
ISBN 978-3-8482-2634-4

Kommunikation in der Produktion
ISBN 978-3-8482-5126-1

Rollen & Verantwortlichkeiten in der Produktion
ISBN 978-3-7322-5290-9

5 rules of production
ISBN 978-3-7357-3675-8

Communication in the production
ISBN 978-3-7347-2963-8

Das Werker Entwicklungs- Programm „WEP"
ISBN 978-3-7494-8058-6

5 Fragen an den Interim Manager
ISBN 978-3-7519-5860-8

and more

interim management for beginners